JAMES DOBSON

Raising Teenagers Right

POCKET GUIDES™
Tyndale House Publishers, Inc.
Wheaton, Illinois

Adapted from *Dr. Dobson Answers Your Questions,* copyright 1982 by James C. Dobson, Tyndale House Publishers, Inc.

Excerpts from James C. Dobson, *Preparing for Adolescence,* copyright 1978, Vision House Publishers, Santa Ana, CA 92705, used by permission.

Pocket Guide is a trademark of Tyndale House Publishers, Inc.
Library of Congress Catalog Card Number 88-50919
ISBN 0-8423-5139-6

Printed in the United States of America

95 94 93 92

9 8 7 6

CONTENTS

INTRODUCTION

During the summer of 1981, my family joined two others on a white water rafting trip down the beautiful Rogue River in Oregon. Those three days of churning water and blistering sun turned out to be one of the most exciting experiences of our lives . . . and perhaps my last! Just before departing on the journey I was told by our host, Dr. Richard Hosley, that "the river is always boss." Forty-eight hours later I learned what he meant.

Rather than floating on the raft for forty miles in relative serenity and safety, I chose to paddle along behind in a plastic eight-foot canoe. And on the second afternoon, I insisted on rowing into the most treacherous part of the river. It was a bad decision.

Ahead lay a section of water known as the "Coffeepot," so named because the narrowing of the rock-walled banks created an unpredictable, bubbling current that had been known to suck small boats below the surface without warning. In fact, one unfortunate raftsman drowned in that area a few summers ago. Nevertheless, I paddled toward the rapids with confidence (and blissful ignorance).

I seemed to be handling the task quite well for the first few moments, before everything suddenly came unraveled. I was hit unexpectedly by the backwash flowing over a large rock and was unceremoniously thrown into the turbulent water. It seemed like an eternity before I came to the surface, only to find breathing impossible. A bandana that had been around my neck was now plastered across my mouth and was held there by my glasses. By the time I clawed free and gasped for air, another wave hit me in the face, sending half the river into my lungs. I came up coughing and sputtering before taking another unscheduled trip below the surface. By then I was desperate for air and keenly aware that the Coffeepot was only twenty-five yards downstream!

A kind of panic gripped me that I had not experienced since childhood! Although my life jacket probably guaranteed my survival, I definitely considered the possibility that I was drowning. My family and friends watched helplessly from the raft as I bobbed through the rapids into the narrowest section of the river.

Through incredible rowing skill, Dr. Hosley managed to "hold" the raft until I could float alongside and grab the rope that rims the upper exterior structure. Then, as we were thrown from one side of the river to another, I pulled my feet up and sprang off the rocks and into the raft, avoiding a crushing blow against the vertical walls of the bank. I can assure you that I rode for several miles in the safety of the raft before moving a muscle!

The only lasting casualty of the experience is a matter of collegiate pride. Dr. Hosley was wearing a shirt with his beloved Stanford University named across the front. It survived the trip. But somewhere on the bottom of the Rogue River in shame and dishonor lies a watersoaked hat bearing the logo of the University of Southern California. It was a sad moment in the historic rivalry between the two alma maters!

After the crisis had passed, I reflected on the utter helplessness I had felt as the river's toy. My life was totally out of control and nothing could be taken for granted, not even a breath of air. Then my thoughts turned to the similar panic that is expressed so often in my counseling practice and in letters that are sent to my office. I currently receive thousands of letters per day, many of which reflect the same helplessness and lack of control I felt in the Rogue River. In fact, the analogy to "drowning" is certainly appropriate in this context; anxious people often use that precise term to describe the experience of being inundated by the events of life. Either they or their loved ones are involved in drug abuse, infidelity, alcoholism, divorce, physical disabilities, mental illness, adolescent rebellion, or low self-esteem. And immediately downstream are even greater dangers and threats.

THE "RAPIDS" OF ADOLESCENCE

Not all of the people who express this kind of anxiety are adults who have had time to mature and perceive life from a grown-up perspective. Some are children and adolescents who are trying to cope with problems in the best way possible. And for many today, their only alternative seems to be the ultimate self-hatred of suicide. Consider the following letter I received last year from a bewildered young man whom I'll call Roger.

Dear Dr. Dobson:

Hi, I'm 11 years old. I'm going into 6th grade. I just got done reading your book, "Preparing for Adolescence." I want you to know it helped me.

When I was in 5th grade I was going with this girl. She broke up with me. *I had family problems*. [Italics mine.] So I tried to hang myself. Well I got a really bad pain in my neck. Then I got to where I couldn't breathe. I realized I wanted to live. So I yanked the noose off. And now God and I are struggling together.

Love,
Roger

P.S. I didn't go into drugs and I never will. I have been asked but I say no. Some people respect me, others think I'm chicken. I don't care.

Each desperate letter of this nature that I receive represents thousands of individuals with similar problems who do not bother to write. And at the core of their vast reservoir of misery lies the great common denominator of turmoil within the family. (Note Roger's vague reference to his problems at home. One can imagine its pivotal role in his attempted suicide.) The American family is experiencing an unprecedented period of disintegration which threatens the entire superstructure of our society, and we simply *must* take whatever steps are necessary to insure its integrity.

The urgency of this mission has become the predominant passion of my professional life. My greatest desire is to serve the God of my fathers by contributing to the stability and harmony of individual families in every way possible. If I can prevent just *one* child from experiencing the nightmare of parental conflict and divorce and custody hearings and wrenching emotional pain, then my life will not have been lived in vain. If I can snatch a *single* fellow traveler from the turbulent waters that threaten to take him under, then there is purpose and meaning to my work. If I can lead but one lost human being to the personhood of Jesus Christ—the giver of life itself—then I need no other justification for my earthly existence.

That brings us to the book you are about to read, which is a product of the mission I've described. In this instance, however, our purpose has not been to deal with the great crises of life. Rather, our focus has been on the common questions relating to the institutions of parenthood and, specifically, to the rearing of teenagers. The philosophy underlying the recommendations offered is based on the best psychological information now available, in keeping with the commandments and values provided by the Creator Himself.

Finally, I should explain that the material presented herein is taken from a larger book, *Dr. Dobson Answers Your Questions*. In it, I drew literally from my previous writings and recordings by condensing larger discussions into more succinct replies. Portions of seven earlier books were represented in this volume, beginning with *Dare to Discipline* which has appeared in three different editions with a combined total of forty printings, and concluding with *Straight Talk to Men and Their Wives*. Our purpose was to extract frequently asked questions and answers which heretofore had been "buried" deep within the original publications.

I hope you find this book helpful, whether you are currently gasping for air or floating high above the rapids. Thanks for your interest in our work, and may God continue to bless your home.

James Dobson, Ph.D.

CHAPTER

1

Preparing Your Child for Puberty

FATIGUE AND PUBERTY

My thirteen-year-old son has become increasingly lazy in the past couple of years. He lies around the house and will sleep half a day on Saturday. He complains about being tired a lot. Is this typical of early adolescence? How should I deal with it?

It is not uncommon for boys and girls to experience fatigue during the pubertal years. Their physical resources are being invested in a rapid growth process during that time, leaving less energy for other activities. This period doesn't last very long and is usually followed by the most energetic time of life.

I would suggest, first, that you take your son for a routine physical examination to rule out the possibility of a more serious explanation for his fatigue. If it does turn out to be a phenomenon of puberty, as I suspect, you should "go with the flow." See that he gets plenty of rest and sleep. This need is often not met, however, because teenagers feel that they should not have to go to bed as early as they did when they were children. Therefore, they stay up too late and then drag through the next day in a state of exhaustion. Surprisingly, a twelve- or thirteen-year-old person actually needs more rest than when he was nine or ten, simply because of the acceleration in growth.

What I'm saying is that you should let your son sleep on Saturday morning, if possible. It is often difficult for mothers and fathers to permit their overgrown son or daughter to lie in bed until 9:30 A.M., when the grass needs mowing. However, they should know that he is lying in bed because he needs more sleep, and they would be wise to let him get it. *Then* ask him to mow the lawn when he awakens.

Second, the foods your son eats are also very important during this time. His body needs the raw materials with which to construct new muscle cells, bones, and fibers that are in the plans. Hot dogs, donuts, and milkshakes just won't do the job. Again, it is even more important to eat a *balanced* diet during this time.

In summary, your son is turning overnight from a boy to a man. Some of the physical characteristics you are observing are part of that transformation. Do everything you can to facilitate it.[1]

SEXUALITY AND THE ADOLESCENT

When do children begin to develop a sexual nature? Does this occur suddenly during puberty?

No, it occurs long before puberty. Perhaps the most important scientific fact suggested by Freud was his observation that children are not asexual. He stated that sexual gratification begins in the cradle and is first associated with feeding. Behavior during childhood is influenced considerably by sexual curiosity and interest, although the happy hormones do not take full charge until early adolescence. It is not uncommon for a four-year-old to be fascinated by nudity and the sexual apparatus of boys versus girls. This is an important time in the forming of sexual attitudes; parents should be careful not to express shock and extreme disapproval of this kind of curiosity, although they are entitled to inhibit overt sexual activity between children. It is believed that many sexual problems begin as a result of inappropriate training during early childhood.[2]

What are the key characteristics of puberty?

First, the glandular and hormonal influences result in rapid sexual development of the body. This accelerated maturation generates a greatly increased interest in the opposite sex. During the early days of puberty, it is common for a teenager to concentrate on sex most of the time. He is fascinated by this exciting new world and he wants to learn all he can about it. A word of advice might be timely at this point: parents should not be shocked by what they see or hear from a pubescent child; he is liable to say or write nearly anything. The most timid little monosyllabic adolescent can sometimes compose the most astonishing profanity. This kind of sexual exploration should not be considered indicative of moral decay—it typically signals the child's sudden fascination with sex.

Along with the newly acquired interest in sex comes a considerable amount of anxiety and concern. The threat emanates from many related sources. A tense adolescent may repeatedly ask himself scores of questions concerning his sexual development: "Are all these changes supposed to be happening? Is there something wrong with me? Do I have a disease or an abnormality? Does this pain in my breasts mean I have cancer? Will I be sexually adequate? Will the boys laugh at me? Will the girls reject me? Will God punish me for the sexual thoughts I have? Wouldn't it be awful if I became a homosexual? Could I get pregnant without having sexual relations? Do some people fail to mature sexually? Could I be one of those people? Will my modesty be sacrified?" These kinds of fears are almost universal among early adolescents. In fact, it is almost impossible to grow up in our culture without some worry and concern about sexuality.[3]

SEX EDUCATION

Who should teach children about sex and when should that instruction begin?

For those parents who are able to handle the instructional process correctly, the responsibility for sex education should be retained in the home. There is a growing trend for all aspects of education to be taken from the hands of parents (or the role is deliberately forfeited by them). This is unwise. Particularly in the matter of sex education, the best approach is one that begins in early childhood and extends through the years, according to a policy of openness, frankness, and honesty. Only parents can provide this lifetime training.

The child's needs for information and guidance can rarely be met in one massive conversation provided by reluctant parents as their child approaches adolescence. Nor does a concentrated formal educational program outside the home offer the same advantages derived from a *gradual* enlightenment that begins during the third or fourth year of life and reaches a culmination shortly before puberty.[4]

We've been very slow getting around to teach sex education in our family. In fact, our child is eleven now, and we haven't given her any specific instructions. Is it too late, or is there still time to prepare her for adolescence?

Your situation is not ideal, of course, but you should do your best to help your daughter understand what the next few years will bring. Parents should usually plan to end their instructional program before their child enters puberty (the time of rapid sexual development in early adolescence). Puberty usually begins between ten and twelve years of age for girls and between twelve and fourteen for boys. Once this developmental period is entered, teenagers are typically embarrassed by discussions of sex with their parents. Adolescents usually resent adult intrusion during this time, preferring to have the subject of sex ignored at home. We should respect their wishes. We are given but a single decade to provide the proper understanding of human sexuality; after that foundation has been constructed, we can only serve as resources to whom the child can turn if he chooses.[5]

Neither my husband nor I feels comfortable about discussing sex with our children. He thinks the school should supply the information they need, but I feel that it is our responsibility. Must I force myself to talk about this difficult subject?

Despite the desirability of sex education being handled by highly skilled parents, we have to face the fact that many families feel as you do. They are admittedly unqualified and reluctant to do the job. Their own sexual inhibitions make it extremely difficult for them to handle the task with poise and tact. For families such as yours that cannot teach their children the details of human reproduction, there must be outside agencies that will assist them in this important function. It is my firm conviction that the Christian church is in the best position to provide that support for its members, since it is free to teach not only the anatomy and physiology of reproduction, but also the *morality and responsibility* of sex. Unfortunately, most churches are also reluctant to accept the assignment, leaving the public schools as the only remaining resource.[6]

Do you believe in the "double standard," whereby girls are expected to remain virgins while boys are free to experiment sexually?

I most certainly do not. There is no such distinction found in the Bible, which must be the standard by which morality is measured. Sin is sin, whether committed by males or females.

How can I instill a healthy attitude toward sex in my child?

The discipline of adolescent sexual drives has never been easy, even when society was supportive of its importance. But our culture now agitates against traditional morality. Our youngsters are immersed in a world which is questioning the value of premarital virginity; even marital fidelity is less important than it was a few years ago. The message of sexual freedom is being preached with evangelistic fervor in the theater, television, magazines, radio, and in the recording industry. Sex is used to sell everything from toothpaste to breakfast cereal.

Children and adolescents are not deaf to these voices. Their society is overwhelmingly preoccupied with sex and their parents cannot divorce them from its influence. How can concerned families counterbalance these forces that surround their impressionable children?

The most fundamental element in teaching morality can be achieved through a healthy parent-child relationship during the early years of the child's life. The obvious hope is that the adolescent will respect and appreciate his parents enough to believe what they say and accept what they recommend.

Unfortunately, however, this loyalty to parents is often an insufficient source of motivation. It is my firm conviction that children should be taught ultimate loyalty to God. We should make it clear that the merciful God of love whom we serve is also a God of wrath. If we choose to defy His moral laws we will suffer certain consequences. God's spiritual laws are as inflexible as His physical laws. If a man jumps from the top of a twenty-story building he will die as his body crashes to the earth below; likewise, the willful violation of God's commandments is equally disastrous, for "the wages of sin is death" (Rom. 6:23). An adolescent who understands this truth is more likely to live a moral life in the midst of an immoral society.

One further comment may be relevant. I hope to give my daughter a small, gold key on her tenth birthday. It will be attached to a chain to be worn around her neck, and will represent the key to her heart. Perhaps she will give that key to one man only—the one who will share her love through the remainder of her life.[7]

How do you feel about sex education in the public shools, as it is typically handled?

For the children of Christian families or others with firm convictions about moral behavior, an acceptable sex education program must consist of two elements. First the anatomy and physiology of reproduction should be taught. Second, moral attitudes and responsibilities related to sex must be discussed. *These components should never be separated as long as the issue of morality is considered important!* Sexual sophistication without sexual responsibility is sexual disaster! To explain all the mechanics of reproduction without teaching the proper attitudes and controls is like giving a child a loaded gun without showing him how to use it. Nevertheless, this second responsibility is often omitted or minimized in the public school setting.

Despite their wish to avoid the issue of morality, teachers of sex education find it almost impossible to remain neutral on the subject. Students will not allow them to conceal their viewpoint. "But what do you think about premarital intercourse, Mr. Burgess?" If Mr. Burgess refuses to answer this question, he has inadvertently told the students that there is no definite right or wrong involved. By not taking a stand for morality he has endorsed promiscuity. The issue appears arbitrary to his students, rendering it more likely that their intense biological desires will get satisfied.

I would like to stress the fact that I am not opposed to sex education in the public schools – provided both elements of the subject are presented properly. However, I don't want my children taught sex technology by a teacher who is either neutral or misinformed about the consequences of immorality. It would be preferable that Junior would learn his concepts in the streets than for a teacher to stand before a class, having all the dignity and authority invested in him by the school and society, and tell his impressionable students that traditional morality is either unnecessary or unhealthy. Unless the schools are prepared to take a definite position in favor of sexual responsibility (and perhaps the social climate prevents their doing so), some other agency should assist concerned parents in the provision of sex education for their children. As indicated earlier, churches could easily provide this service for society. The YMCA, YWCA, or other social institutions might also be helpful at this point. Perhaps there is no objective that is more important to the future of our nation than the teaching of moral discipline to the most recent generation of Americans.[8]

AVOIDING ADOLESCENT STRESS

Is it really that important to discuss puberty with my child?

At the risk of being redundant, I feel I must repeat a word of advice offered in my book *Hide or Seek*. I stressed there the importance of preparing the preteenager for adolescence. We know, as parents, that the teen years can be extremely distressing and tense, yet we typically keep that information to ourselves. We fail to brace our children properly for the social pressures and physical changes that await their arrival at puberty. Instead, we send them skipping unsuspectingly into this hazardous terrain, like Little Red Riding Hood dancing merrily down the path with a basket of goodies. If that sweet child's parents had warned her about the Big Bad Wolf, she might have noticed that Grandmummie had grown hairier and produced a tail since they last met. (I've often wondered what that old woman must have looked like, considering she could have been confused with a wolf by a member of her own family.) Instead, naive Little Red practically climbed into Lobo's mouth to examine the size of his (her) fangs and was saved by the woodsman at the last second. In real life, unfortunately, the story does not usually end with a dramatic rescue and a "happy ever after" conclusion.

It should be our purpose to help our kids avoid the adolescent "wolves" that threaten to devour them. Great strides can be made in that direction by taking the preteenager away from home for at least one day for the purpose of discussing the experiences and events that are approaching. These conversations are most productive when scheduled immediately prior to puberty and should be planned carefully to expose the major "stress points" of adolescence.[9]

I know it is my responsibility to teach Ricky, my preteenager, the essentials of reproduction and sex education before he reaches adolescence. But what else should I tell him?

I have prepared a six-cassette tape album entitled, "Preparing for Adolescence," which deals with topics you will want to to discuss. It is my understanding that this series, published by One Way Library, is one of the best-selling tape albums in America today. Why? Simply because the preadolescent is in such a delicate period of life; nevertheless, very few Christian materials have been directed to his specific needs or expressed in language he can comprehend.

The subjects discussed on the six tapes are listed below, which will also provide suggested topics for parents who want to handle the assignment without recorded assistance.

Tape #1 *The Canyon of Inferiority.* This tape discusses the widespread feelings of inferiority among adolescents and why this low self-esteem occurs. It also suggests how to overcome a lack of confidence. Older teenagers should hear this tape as well.

Tape #2 *Conformity in Adolescence.* This second tape reveals the enormous peer pressure experienced during the teenage years. The dangers of group pressure, including drug abuse and alcoholism, are discussed.

Tape #3 *Explanation of Puberty.* This tape is devoted to an in-depth presentation of the physical changes that often frighten the uninformed child. Fears of abnormality, disease, and freakishness (such as very early or late development) are pacified and relieved. Sexual development is also discussed openly and confidently, including an explanation of menstruation, nocturnal emissions, masturbation, size of breasts and reproductive organs, etc. This understanding can prevent years of suffering and unnecessary worry if presented at the proper time.

Tape #4 *The Meaning of Love*. This tape is designed to clarify the ten most common misconceptions about romantic love. Many adults will enjoy this discussion.

Tape #5 *The Search for Identity*. This tape serves as a wrap-up presentation, discussing the other emotions that so frequently accompany adolescence.

Tape #6 *Rap Session*. This final tape is perhaps the most interesting presentation in the album. Four teenagers gathered for a rap session in my home, discussing their early experiences as an adolescent. Their previous fears, embarrassment, and anxieties are exposed in an open and lively interaction.

I have not wanted this answer to sound like an advertisement for my own creative effort, although I suppose that is what it is. However, I have offered this recommendation simply because the preteenager needs more attention than he is getting. The tranquillity of his next six or eight years may depend on the orientation he is given at the gateway to adolescence. Thus, whether my tapes are used or not, an effort should be made by parents, teachers, and churches to pacify the fears and doubts and pressures of the teen experiences. (The "Preparing for Adolescence" album can be obtained at many Christian bookstores.)[10]

CHAPTER

2

Self-Doubt and the Adolescent Blues

THE CRUCIAL JUNIOR HIGH YEARS

What is the most difficult period of adolescence, and what is behind the distress?

The thirteenth and fourteenth years commonly are the most difficult twenty-four months in life. It is during this time that self-doubt and feelings of inferiority reach an all-time high, amidst the greatest social pressures yet experienced. An adolescent's worth as a human being hangs precariously on peer group acceptance, which can be tough to garner. Thus, relatively minor evidences of rejection or ridicule are of major significance to those who already see themselves as fools and failures. It is difficult to overestimate the impact of having no one to sit with on the school-sponsored bus trip, or of not being invited to an important event, or of being laughed at by the "in" group, or of waking up in the morning to find seven shiny new pimples on your bumpy forehead, or of being slapped by the girl you thought had liked you as much as you liked her. Some boys and girls consistently face this kind of social catastrophe throughout their teen years. They will never forget the experience.

Dr. Urie Bronfenbrenner, eminent authority on child development at Cornell University, told a Senate committee that the junior high years are probably the most crucial to the development of a child's mental health. It is during this period of self-doubt that the personality is often assaulted and damaged beyond repair. Consequently, said Bronfenbrenner, it is not unusual for healthy, happy children to enter junior high school, but then emerge two years later as broken, discouraged teenagers.

I couldn't agree more emphatically with Bronfenbrenner's opinion at this point. Junior high school students are typically brutal to one another, attacking and slashing a weak victim in much the same way a pack of wolves kills and devours a deformed caribou. Few events stir my righteous indignation more than seeing a vulnerable child–fresh from the hand of the Creator in the morning of his life–being taught to hate himself and despise his physical body and wish he had never born.[1]

LOOKS: HOW MUCH DO THEY MATTER?

What do teenagers most often dislike about themselves?

If you asked ten teenagers what they are most unhappy about, eight of them would be dissatisfied with some feature of their bodies. Did you know that about 80 percent of the teenagers in our society don't like the way they look? *Eighty percent!* They feel ugly and unattractive, and they think about that problem most of the time. They also believe that the opposite sex doesn't like them. The girls feel too tall and the boys feel too short, or they feel too fat or too thin, or they're worried about the pimples on their faces or about the freckles on their noses or the color of their hair, or they think their feet are too big or they don't like their fingernails.

No matter how minor the problem is, it can create great anxieties and depression. Most teenagers examine themselves carefully in the mirror to see how much damage has been done by Mother Nature, and they don't like what they see. Since none of us is perfect, they usually find something about themselves that they don't like. Then they worry and fret about it, wishing they didn't have that flaw. Can you imagine being depressed and miserable over something as silly as having a nose that is a fraction of an inch longer than you think it should be?[2]

TEASING: PROCEED WITH CAUTION

I know children can be hateful and mean, especially to the handicapped child or one who is "different." This seems terribly destructive to kids who are especially vulnerable to ridicule. Do you agree that adults are responsible to intercede when a child is being attacked by his peers?

I certainly do and I am well aware of the dangers you described. In fact, I lived it. When I was approximately eight years old, I attended a Sunday school class as a regular member. One morning a visitor entered our class and sat down. His name was Fred, and I can still see his face. More important, I can still see Fred's ears. They were curved in the shape of a reversed C, and protruded noticeably. I was fascinated by the shape of Fred's unusual ears because they reminded me of jeep fenders (we were in deep into World War II at the time). Without thinking of Fred's feelings, I pointed out his strange feature to my friends, who all thought Jeep Fenders was a terribly funny name for a boy with bent ears. Fred seemed to think it was funny, too, and he chuckled along with the rest of us. Suddenly, Fred stopped laughing. He jumped to his feet, red in the face (and ears), and rushed to the door crying. He bolted into the hall and ran from the building. Fred never returned to our class.

I remember my shock over Fred's violent and unexpected reaction. You see, I had *no* idea that I was embarrassing him by my little joke. I was a sensitive kid and often defended the underdog, even when I was a youngster. I would *never* have hurt a visitor on purpose – and that is precisely my point. Looking back on the episode, I hold my teachers and my parents responsible for that event. They should have told me what it feels like to be laughed at . . . especially for something different about your body. My mother, who was very wise with children, has since admitted that she should have taught me to feel for others. And as for the Sunday school leaders, I don't remember what their curriculum consisted of at that time, but what better content could they have presented than the *real* meaning of the commandment, "Love thy neighbor as thyself"?[3]

HELP YOUR CHILD COMPENSATE

I have an adolescent daughter who lacks confidence and self-respect. What can I do to help her?

Let me give you several suggestions that may help your daughter.

1. Help your daughter recognize that she is not alone.

When your daughter goes to school tomorrow, tell her to watch the students who are coming and going. Some will be smiling and laughing and talking and carrying their books and playing baseball. Unless you take a second look, you'd never know they had a care in the world. But I assure you, many of them have the same concerns that trouble your daughter. They reveal these doubts by being very shy and quiet or by being extremely angry and mean or by being silly or by being afraid to participate in a game or contest or by blushing frequently or by acting proud and "stuck-up." She'll soon learn to recognize the signs of inferiority, and then she'll know that it is a *very* common disorder! Once she fully comprehends that others feel as she does, she *should never again* feel alone. It will give her more confidence to know that everyone is afraid of embarrassment and ridicule – that we're all sitting in the same leaky boat, trying to plug the watery holes.

2. Encourage your daughter to face her problem.

Look squarely at the thought that keeps gnawing at her from the back of her mind or from deep within her heart. It would be a good idea for her to make a list of all the things she most dislikes about herself. Nobody is going to see this paper except the people to whom she chooses to show it, so she can be completely honest. When she's finished, tell her to go back through the list and put a check mark by those items that worry her the most – the problems she spends the most time thinking and fretting about. Then it would be a good idea for her to select someone she trusts, a person in whom she has confidence. This should be an adult who understands the problems of young people. Perhaps it will be you – or her teacher or counselor or pastor. She can take her list to that trusted leader and go over it with him or her, discussing each one of her problems. It's best if she talks openly about her feelings, asking her friend to make suggestions about changing the things that concern her.

It is very likely that many of the problems she faces have been conquered by other people, and she may be able to profit from their experience also. In other words, there could be an easy solution available. Maybe she doesn't have to go through life struggling with the same concerns that have troubled other people.

But how will she handle the remaining items

on her list? What can she do with the more difficult problems that defy solution? *It would be wise to remember that the best way to have a healthy mind is to learn to accept those things which you cannot change.* There will always be circumstances which we wish we could rearrange or remove. However, the happiest people in the world are not those who have no problems, but the people who have learned to live with those things that are less than perfect.

Let me suggest, then, that your daughter take her remaining list of "unsolvable problems" to a private place where a small fire will not be dangerous. Perhaps she would like to have her counselor-friend present for this ceremony. She can burn that paper as a symbol to God that the problems are now His. Her prayers should contain this message to Him (stated in her own words):

> Dear Jesus, I am bringing all my problems and worries to you tonight, because you are my best friend. You already know about my strengths and weaknesses, because You made me. That's why I'm burning this paper now. It's my way of saying that I'm giving my life to you . . . with my good qualities along with my shortcomings and failures. I'm asking you to use me in whatever way You wish. Make me the kind of person You want me to be. And from this moment forward, I'm not going to worry about my imperfections.

The Bible teaches us to reveal this humble dependence on the Lord, and He will honor it!

3. Help your daughter compensate for her weaknesses.

Compensation may be a ten-dollar word, but it has a very simple meaning. It means *to make up for your weaknesses by concentrating on your strengths*—in other words, to *compensate* for your weaknesses. Returning to the unsolvable problems on your daughter's list that bother her the most, she can *balance* those weak areas by excelling in some other abilities.

Not everybody can be the best-looking person in school. If this is your daughter's situation, she can say, "All right, so what? There are a lot of other people in the same boat, and it doesn't really matter. My worth doesn't depend on the arrangement of my body. I'll put my effort into something that will help me feel good about myself. I'll be the best trumpet player in the band, or I'll succeed in my part-time job, or I'll raise rabbits for fun and profit, or I'll make good grades in school, or I'll see how many friends I can make, or I'll learn how to play basketball as well as possible, or I'll become a good pianist or drummer, or I'll just see how pleasant a personality I can develop (that's one that nearly everybody can work on), or I'll learn to play tennis, or I'll become a seamstress, or I'll draw or paint and express myself through art, or I'll write poetry or short stories, or I'll become a good cook." Or maybe she could become highly skilled at entertaining small children and become well-trained as a child-care worker.

4. Impress on your daughter the value of genuine friends.

When you know that other people like you, it's much easier to accept yourself. You don't have to be beautiful or highly intelligent or wealthy in order to be liked by other people. "The best way to *have* a friend is to *be* a good friend to others." That's a very old proverb, but it's still very true.

How can your daughter make new friends quickly and easily? It will help her to remember that the people she deals with every day have exactly the same problems I've been discussing. Understanding that fact will help her know how to get along with them and earn their respect. She'll never want to make fun of other people or ridicule them. Instead, she'll want to let them know she respects and accepts them, and that they are important to her.

Your daughter will be surprised at how many friends she can make by being understanding, by "covering" for other people when they make a mistake, by standing up for them when others are trying to make them feel foolish. She'll find that this sensitivity leads to friendship, which leads to greater self-confidence.

One of the most important responsibilities in the Christian life is to care about other people—to smile at them and to be a friend of the friendless. You see, God wants to use you and your daughter to help His other children who feel inferior. He said, "Inasmuch as you do it to the least of these my brethren, you are doing it unto me!" If your daughter starts living this kind of Christian life as recommended by the Bible, I know she'll find that her own self-confidence will grow, and that God will bless her for it. The Lord honors those who obey Him.[4]

PEER PRESSURE AND CONFORMITY

Why is social pressure so great during adolescence? Why are my teenagers so afraid of being rejected by the group?

The answer to these questions goes back to the subject of inferiority.

You see, when you feel worthless and foolish—when you don't like yourself—then you are more frightened by the threat of ridicule or rejection by your friends. You become more sensitive about being laughed at. You lack the confidence to be different. Your problems seem bad enough without making them worse by defying the wishes of the majority. So you dress the way they tell you to dress, and you talk the way they tell you to talk, and all your ideas are the group's ideas. Your great desire is to behave in the "safest" way possible. These behaviors all have one thing in common: They result from feelings of inferiority.

Dean Martin once said, "Show me a man who doesn't know the meaning of the word 'fear' and I'll show you a dummy who gets beat up a lot!" In this case, however, it's not really a fear of getting "beat up" but a fear that the group is going to reject you—the fear of not being invited to a party . . . the fear of being disliked . . . the fear of failure.[5]

Is there anything wrong with letting my son "run with the pack"? Isn't it normal

for him to do what everyone else is doing?

The reason conformity is so dangerous is that it can cause your son to do things that he knows are wrong. This is what happens when he doesn't have the courage to be different from his friends.

Suppose he's in a car with four other young people, each about fifteen years old. They're driving around at night, looking for fun, when the driver reaches into his pocket and retrieves a bottle with some little red pills in it. He takes one pill and pops it in his mouth, and then hands the bottle to the guy sitting by the door. He laughs and takes a pill before handing the bottle to the three fellows in the back seat. Your son is the last one to be handed the bottle, and all four of his friends have taken the pills.

As it is handed to him, what is he going to say? He knows that those capsules are called "reds," and that they are very harmful to the body. He doesn't want to take them, but he doesn't want to be laughed at either. He hesitates a moment, which causes the fellow beside him to say, "Come on, Sissy. Whatsa matter? You scared? Hey guys, we've got a Mama's boy back here! He's afraid Daddy will find out. Who would have thought that Jackie-Boy was a big chicken! Come on, Baby Face. Try it, you'll like it!" The pressure is enormous.

If your son tries it once to see what it's like, he'll find that the next time drugs are offered it'll be a little easier to take them because he's done it before. Then he may become seriously hooked on narcotics, all because of the pressure of conformity. This explains the most important reason why drugs are being used by teenagers every day throughout this country.

Other harmful behaviors can also be traced to the pressure of conformity. Why do you suppose teenage alcoholism is such a serious problem in this country? Why else would cigarettes continue to be smoked by young people, even though they know that the habit has been proven to shorten life, contaminate the lungs, increase the risk of cancer, and damage the blood vessels?

It will be helpful for your son to think about these issues *before* he faces a crisis with his friends. They are under the same pressure that he feels. They're tempted to take drugs or smoke or drink for the same reason he is – simply because they're afraid to be different. They're afraid that the next time their admired friend (the one who owns the car) decides to pick up some guys for a joyride, he won't include them because they're not much fun to be with.

How much better it is for a teenager to show that he has confidence in himself when the pressure is greatest. He can say, "If you guys want to do something crazy, go ahead. But I think it's stupid!" That's not being childish. That's a way of showing that he has the courage to oppose the group when they're wrong.

Most teenagers respect a guy or girl who has the courage to be his own person, even when being mocked and teased. An individual with this kind of confidence often becomes a leader. He has shown that he doesn't feel as inferior as the other followers. He's not made of putty inside. Instead, he has the guts to stand up for what he knows is right.

And one other thing: He is likely to influence others who are looking for that one friend who will increase their confidence. He might make it possible for someone else to oppose peer pressure too.[6]

CHAPTER
3

Discipline Dos and Don'ts

COPING WITH ADOLESCENT ANGER

Our fifteen-year-old son literally seethes with hostility at home—at his mother and me—at his sisters—at the world. Believe me, we have done nothing to provoke this anger, and I don't understand what has caused it. But other parents of teens report the same problem. Why are so many adolescents angry at their parents and family? Sometimes they seem to hate the people who love them the most!

At least part of the answer to that question can be explained by the "in-between" status of teenagers. They live in an era when they enjoy neither the privileges of adulthood nor the advantages of childhood. Consider the plight of the average fifteen-year-old. All of the highly advertised adult privileges and vices are forbidden to him because he is "too young." He can't drive or marry or enlist or drink or smoke or work or leave home. And his sexual desires are denied gratification at a time when they scream for release. The only thing he is permitted to do, it seems, is stay in school and read his dreary textbooks. This is an overstatement, of course, but it is expressed from the viewpoint of the young man or woman who feels disenfranchised and insulted by society. Much of the anger of today's youth is generated by their perception of this injustice.

There is another side to this issue of adolescent volatility. I'm now convinced that the hormonal changes occurring in a developing body may be more important to feelings than we thought earlier. Just as emotions are set on edge by premenstrual tension, menopause, and extreme fatigue, it is entirely possible that the adolescent experience is largely hormonal as well. How else can we explain the ***universality*** of emotional instability during these years? Having watched thousands of children sail from childhood to early adolescence, it still amazes me to witness textbook characteristics suddenly appearing on schedule as though responding to a preprogrammed computer. In fact, they probably are. I can't prove this hypothesis to be valid, but it is making more sense to me year by year.

All right, so my kid feels disrespected and hostile. I still have to impose some limits and discipline on him, don't I?

Yes, but it is possible to lead teenagers without insulting and antagonizing them unnecessarily. I learned this lesson when I was a junior high school teacher. It became clear to me very early that I could impose all manner of discipline and strict behavioral requirements on my students, *provided* I treated each young person with genuine dignity and respect. I earned their friendship before and after school, during lunch, and through classroom encounters. I was tough, especially when challenged, but never discourteous, mean, or insulting. I defended the underdog and tenaciously tried to build each child's confidence and self-respect. However, I never compromised my standards of deportment. Students entered my classroom without talking each day. They did not chew gum, behave disrespectfully, curse, or stab one another with ball point pens. I was clearly the captain of the ship, and I directed it with military zeal.

The result of this combination of kindness and firm discipline stands as one of the most pleasant memories of my professional life. I *loved* my students and had every reason to believe that I was loved in return. I actually missed them on weekends (a fact my wife never quite understood). At the end of the final year when I was packing my books and saying good-bye, there were twenty-five or thirty teary-eyed kids who hung around my gloomy room for several hours and finally stood sobbing in the parking lot as I drove away. And yes, I shed a few tears of my own that day. (Please forgive this self-congratulatory paragraph. I haven't bothered to tell you about my failures, which are far less interesting.)[1]

CONFRONTATION: A CASE STUDY

My son, Brian, is now fourteen years old and he has suddenly entered a period of rebellion like nothing I've ever seen. He is breaking rules right and left and he seems to hate the entire family. He becomes angry when his mother and I try to discipline him, of course, but even during more tranquil times he seems to resent us for merely being there. Last Friday night he arrived home an hour beyond his deadline but refused to explain why he was late or to make apologetic noises. We are in the midst of a nightmare I *never* anticipated when he was younger.

This is my question. I would like you to tell me exactly how to approach this situation, even role-playing my task of confronting him. I need to know what to say when that moment arrives.

Certainly. I would recommend that you invite Brian out to breakfast on a Saturday morning, leaving the rest of the family at home. It would be best if this event could occur during a relatively tranquil time, certainly not in the midst of a hassle or intergenerational battle. Admit that you have some important matters to discuss with him which can't be communicated adequately at home, but don't "tip your hand" before Saturday morning. Then at the appropriate moment during breakfast convey the following messages (or an adaptation thereof):

A. Brian, I wanted to talk to you this morning because of the changes that are taking place in you and in our home. We both know that the past few weeks have not been very pleasant. You have been angry most of the time and have become disobedient and rude. And your mother and I haven't done so well either. We've become irritable and we've said things that we've regretted later. This is not what God wants of us as parents, or of you as our son. There has to be a more creative way of solving our problems. That's why we're all here.

B. As a place to begin, Brian, I want you to understand what is happening. You have gone into a new period of life known as adolescence. This is the final phase of childhood, and it is often a very stormy and difficult few years. Nearly everyone on earth goes through these rough years during their early teens, and you are right on schedule at this moment. Many of the problems you face today were predictable from the day you were born, simply because growing up has never been an easy thing to do. There are even greater pressures on kids today than when we were young. I've said that to tell you this: we understand you and love you as much as we ever did, even though the past few months have been difficult in our home.

C. What is actually taking place, you see, is that you have had a taste of freedom. You are tired of being a little boy who was told what to wear and when to go to bed and what to eat. That is a healthy attitude which will help you grow up. However, now you want to be your own boss and make your own decisions without interference from anyone. Brian, you will get what you want in a very short time. You are fourteen now, and you'll soon be fifteen and seventeen and nineteen. You will be grown up in a twinkling of an eye, and we will no longer have any responsibility for you. The day is coming when you will marry whomever you wish, go to whatever school you choose, select the profession or job that suits you. Your mother and I will not try to make those decisions for you. We will respect your adulthood. Furthermore, Brian, the closer you get to those days, the more freedom we plan to give you. You have more privileges now than you had last year, and that trend will continue. We will soon set you free, and you will be accountable only to God and yourself.

D. But, Brian, you must understand this message: you are not grown yet. During the past few weeks, you have wanted your mother and me to leave you alone – to let you stay out half the night if you chose – to fail in school – to carry no responsibilty at home. And you have "blown up" whenever we have denied even your most extreme demands. The truth of the matter is, you have wanted us to grant you twenty-year-old freedom during the fourteenth year, although you still expect to have your shirts ironed and your meals fixed and your bills paid. You have wanted the best of both worlds with none of the responsibilities. So what are we to do? The easiest thing would be for us to let you have your way. There would be no hassles and no conflict and no more frustration. Many parents of fourteen-year-old sons and daughters have done just that. But we must not yield to this temptation. You are not ready for that complete independence, and we would be showing hatred for you (instead of love) if we surrendered at this time. We would regret our mistake for the rest of our lives, and you would soon blame us, too. And as you know, you have two younger sisters who are watching you very closely, and must be protected from the things you are teaching them.

E. Besides, Brian, God has given us a responsibility as parents to do what is right for you, and He is holding us accountable for the way we do that job. I want to read you an important passage from the Bible which describes a father named Eli who did not discipline and correct his two unruly teenage sons. (Read the dramatic story from *The Living Bible,* 1 Samuel 2:12-17, 22-25, 27-34; 3:11-14; 4:1-3 and 10-22.) It is very clear that God was angry at Eli for permitting his sons to be disrespectful and disobedient. Not only did He allow the sons to be killed in battle, but He also punished their father for not accepting his parental responsibilities. This assignment to parents can be found throughout the Bible: mothers and fathers are expected to train their children and discipline them when required. What I'm saying is that God will not hold us blameless if we let you behave in ways that are harmful to yourself and others.

F. That brings us to the question of where we go from this moment. I want to make a pledge to you, here and now: your mother and

I intend to be more sensitive to your needs and feelings than we've been in the past. We're not perfect, as you well know, and it is possible that you will feel we have been unfair at one time or another. If that occurs, you can express your views and we will listen to you. We want to keep the door of communication standing wide open between us. When you seek a new privilege, I'm going to ask myself this question, "Is there any way I can grant this request without harming Brian or other people?" If I can permit what you want in good conscience, I will do so. I will compromise and bend as far as my best judgment will let me.

G. But hear this, Brian. There will be a few matters that cannot be compromised. There will be occasions when I will have to say no. And when those times come, you can expect me to stand like the Rock of Gibraltar. No amount of violence and temper tantrums and door slamming will change a thing. In fact, if you choose to fight me in those remaining rules, then I promise that you will lose dramatically. Admittedly you're too big and grown up to spank, but I can still make you uncomfortable. And that will be my goal. Believe me, Brian, I'll lie awake nights figuring how to make you miserable. I have the courage and the determination to do my job during these last few years you are at home, and I intend to use all of my resources for this purpose, if necessary. So it's up to you. We can have a peaceful time of cooperation at home, or we can spend this last part of your childhood in unpleasantness and struggle. Either way, you *will* arrive home when you are told, and you *will* carry your share of responsibility in the family and you *will* continue to respect your mother and me.

H. Finally, Brian, let me emphasize the message I gave you in the beginning. We love you more than you can imagine, and we're going to remain friends during this difficult time. There is so much pain in the world today. Life involves disappointment and loss and rejection and aging and sickness and ultimately death. You haven't felt much of that discomfort yet, but you'll taste it soon enough. So with all that heartache outside our door, let's not bring more of it on ourselves. We need each other. We need you, and believe it or not, you still need us occasionally. And that, I suppose, is what we wanted to convey to you this morning. Let's make it better from now on.

I. Do you have things that need to be said to us?

The content of this message should be modified to fit individual circumstances and the needs of particular adolescents. Furthermore, the responses of children will vary tremendously from person to person. An "open" boy or girl may reveal his deepest feelings at such a moment of communication, permitting a priceless time of catharsis and ventilation. On the other hand, a stubborn, defiant, proud adolescent may sit immobile with head downward. But if your teenager remains stoic or hostile, at least the cards have been laid on the table and parental intentions explained.[2]

You have stated that you do not favor spanking a teenager. What would you do to encourage the cooperation of my fourteen-year-old who deliberately makes a nuisance of himself? He throws his clothes around, refuses to help out with any routine tasks in the house, and pesters his little brother perpetually.

I would seek to find a way to link his behavior to something important to the fourteen-year-old, such as privileges or even money. If he receives an allowance, for example, this money could provide an excellent tool with which you can generate a little motivation. Suppose he is given two dollars a week. That maximum can be taxed regularly for violation of predetermined rules. For example, each article of clothing left on the floor might cost him a dime. A deliberate provocation of his brother would subtract a quarter from his total. Each Saturday he would receive the money remaining from the taxation of the last week. This system comforms to the principle behind all adolescent discipline: give the individual reason for obeying other than the simple fact that he was told to do so.[3]

I would like to hear your views about disciplining a teenager, especially since you say spanking him is neither wise nor productive.

Your only tool of discipline is to manipulate your teenager's environmental circumstances in moments of confrontation. You have the keys to the family automobile and can allow your son or daughter to use it (or be chauffeured in it). You may grant or withhold privileges, including permission to go to a party. You control the family purse and can choose to share it or loan it or dole it or close it. And you can "ground" your adolescent or deny him the use of the telephone or television for awhile.

Now obviously, these are not very influential "motivators," and are at times totally inadequate for the situation at hand. After we have appealed to reason and cooperation and family loyalty, all that remains are relatively weak methods of "punishment." We can only link behavior of our kids with desirable and undesirable consequences and hope the connection will be of sufficient influence to elicit their cooperation.

If that sounds pretty wobbly-legged, let me admit what I am implying: a willful, angry sixteen-year-old boy or girl *can* win a confrontation with his or her parents today, if worse comes to worst. The law leans ever more in the direction of emancipation of the teenager. He can leave home in many areas and avoid being returned. He can drink and smoke pot and break many other civil laws before he is punished by society. His girlfriend can obtain birth control pills in many states without her parents' knowledge or permission. And if that fails, she can slip into a clinic for an unannounced abortion. Very few "adult" privileges and vices can be denied a teenager who has the passion for independence and a will to fight.

How different was the situation when Billy-Joe was raised on the farm in days of old, living perhaps eight or ten miles by horseback from the home of his nearest contemporary. His dad, Farmer Brown, impressed by his own authority, could "talk sense" to his rebellious boy without the interference of outside pressures. There is no doubt that it was much easier for father and son to come to terms while sitting on a plow at the far end of Forgotten Field.

But today, every spark of adolescent discontent is fanned into a smoldering flame. The grab for the teen dollar has become big business, with enticing magazines, record companies, radio, television, and concert entrepreneurs to cater to each youthful whim. And, of course, masses of high school students congregate idly in the city and patronize those obliging companies. They have become a force to be considered.

Unless teenagers have an inner tug toward cooperation and responsibility, the situation can get nasty very quickly. But where does that voice of restraint originate? It has been my contention that the early years of childhood are vital to the establishment of respect between generations. Without that kind of foundation—without a touch of awe in the child's perception of his parent—then the balance of power and control is definitely shifted toward the younger combatant. I would be doing a disservice to my readers if I implied otherwise.[4]

STRICTNESS – IT WORKS IN THE CLASSROOM

I have observed that elementary school and junior high school students, even high schoolers, tend to admire strict teachers. Why is this true?

Yes, the teachers who maintain order *are* often the most respected members of the faculties, provided they aren't mean and grouchy. A teacher who can control a class without being oppressive is almost always loved by her students. One reason is that there is safety in order. When a class is out of control, particularly at the elementary school level, the children are afraid of each other. If the teacher can't make the class behave, how can she prevent a bully from doing his thing? How can she keep the students from ridiculing one of its less able members? Children are not very fair and understanding with each other, and they feel good about having a strong teacher who is.

Second, children love justice. When someone has violated a rule, they want immediate retribution. They admire the teacher who can enforce an equitable legal system, and they find great comfort in reasonable social rules. In contrast, the teacher who does not control her class inevitably allows crime to pay, violating something basic in the value system of children.

Third, children admire strict teachers because chaos is nerve-wracking. Screaming and hitting and wiggling are fun for about ten minutes; then the confusion begins to get tiresome and irritating.

I have smiled in amusement many times as children astutely evaluated the relative disciplinary skills of their teachers. They know how a class should be conducted. I only wish all of their teachers were equally aware of this important attribute.[5]

TEACHING RESPONSIBILITY

How can I acquaint my junior higher with the need for responsible behavior throughout his life? He is desperately in need of this understanding.

The overall objective during the preadolescent period is to teach the child that his actions have inevitable consequences. One of the most serious casualties in a permissive society is the failure to connect those two factors, behavior and consequences. Too often, a three-year-old child screams insults at his mother, but Mom stands blinking her eyes in confusion. A first grader launches an attack on his teacher, but the school makes allowances for his age and takes no action. A ten-year-old is caught stealing candy in a store, but is released to the recognizance of his parents. A fifteen-year-old sneaks the keys to the family car, but his father pays the fine when his son is arrested. A seventeen-year-old drives his Chevy like a maniac and his parents pay for the repairs when he wraps it around a telephone pole. You see, all through childhood, loving parents seem determined to intervene between behavior and consequences, breaking the connection and preventing the valuable learning that could have occurred.

Thus, it is possible for a young man or woman to enter adult life, not really knowing that life bites—that every move we make directly affects our future—that irresponsible behavior eventually produces sorrow and pain. Such a person applies for his first job and arrives late for work three times during his first week; then, when he is fired in a flurry of hot words, he becomes bitter and frustrated. It was the first time in his life that Mom and Dad couldn't come running to rescue him from the unpleasant consequences. (Unfortunately, many American parents still try to "bail out" the grown children even when they are in their twenties and live away from home.) What is the result? This overprotection produces emotional cripples who often develop lasting characteristics of dependency and a kind of perpetual adolescence.

How does one connect behavior with consequences? By being willing to let the child experience a reasonable amount of pain or inconvenience when he behaves irresponsibly. When Jack misses the school bus through his own dawdling, let him walk a mile or two and enter school in midmorning (unless safety factors prevent this). If Janie carelessly loses her lunch money, let her skip a meal. Obviously, it is possible to carry this principle too far, being harsh and inflexible with an immature child. But the best approach is to expect boys and girls to carry the responsibility that is appropriate for their age, and occasionally to taste the bitter fruit that irresponsibility bears.[6]

RUNAWAYS

What would you do if your eighteen-year-old son decided to become a social dropout and run away from home?

It is difficult for anyone to know exactly how he would face a given crisis, but I can tell you what I think would be the best reaction under those circumstances. Without nagging and whining, I would hope to influence the boy to change his mind before he made a mistake. If he could not be dissuaded, I would have to let him go. It is not wise for parents to be too demanding and authoritative with an older teenager; they may force him to defy their authority just to prove his independence and adulthood. Besides this, if they pound on the table, wring their hands, and scream at their wayward son, he will not feel the full responsibility for his own behavior. When Mom and Dad are too emotionally involved with him, he can expect them to bail him out if he runs into trouble. I think it is much wiser to treat the late adolescent like an adult; he's more likely to act like one if he is given the status offered to other adults. The appropriate parental reaction should be: "John, you know I feel you are making a choice that will haunt you for many years. I want you to sit down with me and we will analyze the pros and cons; then the final decision will be yours. I will not stand in your way." John knows that the responsibility is on his shoulders. Beginning in middle adolescence, parents should give a child more and more responsibility each year, so that when he gets beyond their control he will no longer need it.

The Gospel of St. Luke contains an amazingly relevant story of a young dropout. It is commonly known as the parable of the Prodigal Son. Read the story in Luke 15 and then note that it contains several important messages that are highly relevant to our day. First, the father did not try to locate his son and drag him home. The boy was apparently old enough to make his own decision and the father allowed him the privilege of determining his course.

Second, the father did not come to his rescue during the financial stress that followed. He didn't send money. There were no well-meaning church groups that helped support his folly. Note in verses 16 and 17, "No one gave him anything . . . he finally came to his senses" (TLB). Perhaps we sometimes keep our children from coming to their senses by preventing them from feeling the consequences of their own mistakes. When a teenager gets a speeding citation, *he* should pay for it. When he wrecks his car, *he* should have it fixed. When he gets suspended from school, *he* should take the consequences without parental protests to the school. He will learn from these adversities. The parent who is too quick to bail his child out of difficulty may be doing him a disservice.

Third, the father welcomed his son home without belittling him or demanding reparations. He didn't say, "I told you you'd make a mess of things!" or "You've embarrassed your mom and me to death. Everyone is talking about what a terrible son we've raised!" Instead, he revealed the depth of his love by saying, "He was lost and is found!"[7]

CHAPTER

4

Dating, Drugs, and Other Dilemmas

A HEALTHY START IN DATING

I have a fourteen-year-old daughter, Margretta, who wants to date a seventeen-year-old boy. I don't feel good about letting her go, but I'm not sure just how to respond. What should I say to her?

Rather than stamping your foot and screaming, "No! And that's semi-final!" I would work out a reasonable plan for the years ahead and a rationale to support it. You might say, "Margretta, you are fourteen years old, and I understand your new interest in boys. That's the way it's supposed to be. However, you are not ready to handle the pressures that an older boy can put on a girl your age." (Explain what you mean if she asks.)

"Your dad and I want to help you get ready for dating in the future, but there are some in-between steps you need to take. You have to learn how to be 'friends' with boys before you become a 'lover' with one. To do this, you should get acquainted in groups of boys or girls your age. We'll invite them to our house or you can go to the homes of others. Then when you are between fifteen and sixteen, you can begin double-dating to places that are chaperoned by adults. And finally, you can go on single dates sometime during your sixteenth year.

"Your dad and I want you to date and have fun with boys, and we intend to be reasonable about this. But you're not ready to plunge into single dating with a high school senior, and we'll just have to find other ways to satisfy your social needs."[1]

"MY DAUGHTER IS PREGNANT"

My unmarried daughter recently told me that she is three months pregnant. What should be my attitude toward her now?

You cannot reverse the circumstances by being harsh or unloving at this point. Your daughter needs more understanding now than ever before, and you should give it to her if possible. Help her grope through this difficulty and avoid "I told you so" comments. She will face many important decisions in the next few months and she will need a calm, rational mother and father to assist in determining the best path to take. Remember that lasting love and affection often develop between people who have survived a crisis together.[2]

My teenage daughter has admitted having sexual relations with several boys. Since she doesn't believe in God she sees no reason for doing otherwise. What can I tell her?

You might make her aware of the fact that sexual freedom is expensive and most of the bills are paid by women. The natural sex appeal of girls serves as their primary source of bargaining power in the game of life. In exchange for feminine affection and love, a man accepts a girl as his lifetime responsibility—supplying her needs and caring for her welfare. This sexual aspect of the marital agreement can hardly be denied. Therefore, a girl who indiscriminately gives away her basis for exchange has little left with which to bargain. Your daughter might also be reminded of the other expenses that are sometimes imposed by sexual irresponsibility, including those associated with venereal disease, unwanted pregnancies, and fatherless children. By contrast, the biblical concept of morality offers overwhelming advantages for a woman, even if the matter of right and wrong were of no significance. Through moral behavior she is more likely to achieve self-respect, the respect of society, the love of a husband, and provision for the needs of her children. The current move toward common-law (unmarried couples living as man and wife) offers no legal protection and no security to the "wife" involved. Similarly, the new morality is a tragic imposition on the female sex; women satisfy the desires of males while assuming the full responsibilities, risks, and consequences themselves. Then when their youth begins to fade, as inevitably it does, they will find little sympathy from the men who have exploited them.

It would be wise for all girls to understand

this message. Parents have the responsibility to lay the facts before their teenagers in this manner, but the ultimate decision must then rest in their hands.[3]

DRUG USE AND ABUSE

Most teenagers know that drug use is harmful to their bodies and can even kill them. Why, then, do they do it? Are they usually the victims of unscrupulous "pushers" who get them hooked on narcotics?

Not usually. The introduction to drug usage is usually made from friend to friend in a social atmosphere. Marijuana and pills are frequently distributed at parties where a nonuser cannot refuse to participate without appearing square and unsophisticated. Many teenagers would literally risk their lives if they thought their peer group demanded them to do so, and this need for social approval is instrumental in the initiation of most drug habits.[4]

What should parents look for as symptoms of drug abuse?

Listed below are eight physical and emotional symptoms that may indicate substance abuse by your child.

1. Inflammation of the eyelids and nose is common. The pupils of the eyes are either very wide or very small, depending on the kind of drugs internalized.

2. Extremes of energy may be represented. Either the individual is sluggish, gloomy, and

withdrawn, or he may be loud, hysterical, and jumpy.

3. The appetite is extreme—either very great or very poor. Weight loss may occur.

4. The personality suddenly changes; the individual may become irritable, inattentive, and confused, or aggressive, suspicious, and explosive.

5. Body and breath odor is often bad. Cleanliness is generally ignored.

6. The digestive system may be upset—diarrhea, nausea, and vomiting may occur. Headaches and double vision are also common. Other signs of physical deterioration may include change in skin tone and body stance.

7. Needle marks on the body, usually appearing on the arms, are an important symptom. These punctures sometimes get infected and appear as sores and boils.

8. Moral values often crumble and are replaced by new, way-out ideas and values.[5]

Where are the drugs obtained?

Illicit drugs are surprisingly easy to obtain by adolescents. The family medicine cabinet usually offers a handy stockpile of prescription drugs, cough medicines, tranquilizers, sleeping pills, reducing aids, and pain killers. Furthermore, a physician can be tricked into prescribing the desired drugs; a reasonably intelligent person can learn from a medical text the symptoms of diseases which are usually treated with the drug he wants. Prescriptions can also be forged and passed at local pharmacies. Some drugs reach the "street market" after having been stolen from pharmacies, doctors' offices or manufacturers' warehouses. However, the vast majority of drugs are smuggled into this country—perhaps after being manufactured here and sold abroad.[6]

RELIGIOUS BELIEFS

At what age should a child be given more freedom of choice regarding his religious beliefs and practices?

After the middle adolescent years (thirteen to sixteen years), some children resent being told exactly what to believe; they do not want religion "forced down their throats," and should be given more and more autonomy in what they believe. But if the early exposure has been properly conducted, they will have an inner mainstay to steady them. That early indoctrination, then, is the key to the spiritual attitudes they will carry into adulthood.

Despite this need to take a softer approach to spiritual training as the child moves through adolescence, it is *still* appropriate for parents to establish and enforce a Christian standard of behavior in their homes. Therefore, I *would* require my seventeen-year-old to attend church with the family. He should be told, "As long as you are under this roof, we will worship God together as a family. I can't control what you think. That's your business. But I have promised the Lord that we will honor Him in this home, and that includes 'remembering the Sabbath to keep it holy.' "[7]

HOW TO LET GO

The following question was posed by *Family Life Today*, a Christian magazine devoted to family issues and interests:

> **What do you do when your child, at age eighteen or twenty, makes choices quite different from what you had hoped? Parents feel frustrated and embarrassed—at a loss to influence the child they thought had been "trained up in the way he should go" but who is now "departing from it." Parenting begins when a child is born. But does it ever end? Should it? If so, when? And how?**

My answer reprinted below is used by permission of *Family Life Today* magazine (copyright 1982), and was originally published in the March 1982 issue.

> "The process of letting go of our offspring should begin shortly after birth and conclude some twenty years later with the final release and emancipation," said Dobson, who readily admits this is the most difficult assignment parents face. "The release is not a sudden event. In fact, from infancy onward, the parent should do nothing for the child that the child can profit from doing for himself. Refusal to grant appropriate independence and freedom results in rebellion and immaturity—whether during the terrible twos or later in adolescence."

A strong advocate of loving discipline during the early years, Dobson contends that there comes a time when the relationship between generations must change. "By the time a child is eighteen or twenty," he noted, "the parent should begin to relate to his or her offspring more as a peer. This liberates the parent from the responsibility of leadership and the child from the obligation of dependency.

"It is especially difficult for us *Christian* parents to release our children into adulthood because we care so much about the outcome of our training. Fear of rebellion and rejection of our values and beliefs often leads us to retain our authority until it is torn from our grasp. By then, permanent damage may have been done to family relationships."

One of the most difficult times for parents to remain reserved is when their young adult offspring chooses a mate not to the parents' liking. "Though it is painful to permit what you think would be a marital mistake," Dobson warned, "it is unwise to become dictatorial and authoritarian in the matter. If you set yourself against the person your child has chosen to marry, you may struggle with in-law problems the rest of your life.

"If there are well-grounded reasons for opposing a potential marriage, a parent can be honest about those convictions at an opportune moment and in an appropriate manner. But that does not entitle the older generation to badger and nag and criticize those who are trying to make this vitally important decision."

For example, he suggested that in such a situation a parent might say: "I have great concern about what you're doing, and I'm going to express my views to you. Then I'll step aside and allow you to make up your own mind. Here are the areas of incompatibility that I foresee (etc.). . . . I'm going to be praying for you as you seek the Lord's will in this important matter." The most critical ingredient, Dobson concluded, is to make it clear that the decision is "owned" by the offspring—not the parent.

What are the consequences of not handling these crises properly? "Unresolved conflicts during late adolescence have a way of continuing into the adult years," replied Dobson. A recent mail-in survey he conducted revealed that 89 percent of the 2,600 people responding felt that they suffered from long-term strained relationships with their own parents. Forty-four percent complained specifically that their parents had never set them free or granted them adult status.

And, added Dobson, the letters that accompanied the survey responses told incredible stories—of a twenty-three-year-old girl who was regularly spanked for misbehavior and others in mid-life who still did not feel accepted and respected by their parents. "Clearly," he said, "the process of letting go is a very difficult process for *most* parents."

What can a mother or father do if the offspring has gone into openly sinful behavior that violates everything the parent has stood for? And how should they react, for example, when their grown kids forsake family ties and join a "New Age" religious group?

"I have not recommended that parents keep their concerns and opinions to themselves," said Dobson, "especially when eternal issues hang in the balance. There is a time to speak up. But the manner in which the message is conveyed must make it clear that the parents' role is advisory . . . not authoritarian. The ultimate goal is for parents to assure the young person of their continued love and commitment, while speaking directly about the dangers that are perceived. And I repeat, it must be obvious that the responsibility for decision making ultimately rests with the offspring."

Dobson, whose books on family interaction have dominated the "top ten" Christian best-seller lists for many months, mused that his next book will probably be about guilt in parenthood. Referring to Proverbs 22:6, he said he agrees with Dr. John White that the Proverbs are presented as *probabilities*, not *promises:* "Even if we train up a child in the way he should go, he *sometimes* goes his own way! That's why we parents tend to experience tremendous guilt that is often unjustified. Our kids live in a sinful world and they often emulate their peers; despite our teaching to the contrary, God gives each child a free will, and He will not take it from them—nor can we."

Citing several environmental and inborn factors that parents do not control—including individual temperment, peer-group pressures and the innate will of the child—Dobson noted that these combined forces are probably more influential than parental leadership itself. "It is simply unfair to attribute everthing young adults do . . . good or bad . . . to parental skill or ignorance.

"A hundred years ago when a child went wrong, he was written off as a 'bad kid.' Now, any failure or rebellion in the younger generation is blamed on the parents—supposedly reflecting their mistakes and shortcomings. Such a notion is often unjust and fails to acknowledge a young adult's freedom to run his own life."

What attitude, then, should a parent have toward a twenty-one-year-old offspring who insists on living with someone of the opposite sex? "It is difficult to force anything on a person that age, and in fact, a parent shouldn't try," Dobson warned. "But Mom and Dad certainly do not have to pay for the folly."

He noted that the father of the Prodigal Son, symbolizing God's patient love, permitted his son to enter a life of sin. But he didn't send his servants to "bail out" his erring youngest when times got difficult.

"It was the son's choice to go into a sinful life-style, and the father permitted both the behavior and the consequences," Dobson observed. "An over-protective parent who continually sends money to an irresponsible offspring, often breaks this necessary connection between sinful behavior and painful consequences.

"A parent's goal should be to build a friendship with his or her child from the cradle onward," Dobson concluded. "When his task is done properly, both generations can enjoy a lifetime of fellowship after the child has left home and established a family of his own."

After talking with this noted Christian psychologist, one leaves with the impression that parents who once looked with awe and wonder at their bundle of new life may find the delivery of that same child into adulthood two decades later no less a marvel. And just as they could not keep their newborn child in the safety and protection of the womb, they must ultimately permit his or her passage into the grown-up world at the end of childhood. Along the way, wise Christian parents will prayerfully try to influence—but not prolong control over—their maturing child. The rest they leave in the hands of the Creator.

CHAPTER
5
Questions Teens Ask

THE PRESSURE TO CONFORM

I am a teenager and I want to look and dress just like all my friends. My parents tell me I should be an individual and be willing to be different, but I just can't do it. Do *you* understand?

Sure I do. Let me explain why you feel such pressure to be like everyone else. The answer involves feelings of inferiority, which are usually very strong during adolescence. You see, when you feel worthless and foolish—when you don't like yourself—then you are more frightened by the threat of ridicule or rejection by your friends. You become more sensitive about being laughed at. You lack the confidence to be different. Your problems seem bad enough without making them worse by defying the wishes of the majority. So you dress the way they tell you to dress, and you talk the way they tell you to talk, and all your ideas are the group's ideas. You become afraid to raise your hand in class or express your own ideas. Your great desire is to behave in the "safest" way possible. These behaviors all have one thing in common: they result from a lack of self-confidence.

Gradually, your self-respect will return as you become more mature and comfortable with the person God made you to be.[1]

ABOUT ACNE

I am fourteen and I have crummy-looking pimples all over my face. What causes them and what can I do to clear up my skin?

Practically every part of your body is affected in one way or another by the period of change you are now experiencing. Even your skin undergoes major changes, whether you are a boy or a girl. In fact, this is probably the most distressing aspect of all the physical events that take place in early adolescence. A study of two thousand teenagers asked the question, "What do you most dislike about yourself?" Skin problems outranked every other reply by a wide margin.

Skin eruptions occur primarily as a result of an oily substance which is secreted during adolescence. The pores of the skin tend to fill up with this oil and become blocked. Since the oil can't escape, it hardens there and causes pimples or blackheads. You might expect to have these imperfections on your skin for several years, although some cases are milder than others.

When you get numerous pimples and blackheads regularly, the condition is called acne.

If this happens, it will be very important for you to keep your skin clean, minimizing the oil and dirt on your face. We used to think that certain greasy foods and chocolate contributed to the difficulty, but doctors now doubt this relationship. If the problem is severe, as you obviously feel it is, you should ask your parents to take you to a dermatologist, who is a doctor specializing in skin problems. Acne can now be treated effectively in most cases.[2]

WHAT TO DO WHEN YOU FEEL BAD

I am thirteen and I feel miserable about myself. Is there anything I can do?

First, you need to understand that you are not alone. Begin observing the people around you and see if you detect hidden feelings of inferiority. When you go to school tomorrow, quietly watch the students who are coming and going. I assure you, many of them have the same concerns that trouble you. They reveal these doubts by being very shy and quiet, by being extremely angry and mean, by being silly, by being afraid to participate in a game or contest, by blushing frequently, or by acting proud and "stuck-up." You'll soon learn to recognize the signs of inferiority, and then you'll know that it is a *very* common disorder! Once you fully comprehend that others feel as you do, then you *should never again* feel alone. It will give you more confidence to know that everyone is afraid of embarrassment and ridicule—that we're all sitting in the same leaky boat, trying to plug the watery holes. And would you believe, I nearly drowned in that same leaky boat when I was fourteen years old?

Second, I advise you to look squarely at the worries that keep gnawing at you from the back of your mind or from deep within your heart, causing a black cloud to hang over your head day and night. It would be a good idea to get alone, where there is no one to interfere with your thoughts. Then *list* all the things that you most dislike about yourself. Nobody is going to see this paper except the people to whom you choose to show it, so you can be completely honest. Write down everything that has been bothering you. Even admit the characteristics that you dislike, including the tendency to get mad and blow up (if that applies to you).

Identify your most serious problems as best as possible. Do you get frustrated and angry at people and then feel bad later? Or is it your shyness that makes you afraid when you're with other people? Is it your inability to express your ideas—to put your thoughts into words? Is it your laziness, your unkindness to other people, or the way you look? Whatever concerns you, write it down as best you can. Then when you're finished, go back through the list and put a mark by those items that worry you the most—the problems that you spend the most time thinking and fretting about.

Third, think about each item on the list. Give your greatest creative thought to what might be done to change the things you don't like. If you wish, you might share the paper with your pastor, counselor, parent, or someone in whom you have confidence: that person can then help you map out a plan for improvement. You'll feel better for having faced your problems, and you might even find genuine solutions to some of the troublesome matters.

Now, we come to an important step. The key to mental health is being able to accept what you cannot change. After you've done what you can to deal with your problems, I feel you should take the paper on which the most painful items are written, and burn it in a private ceremony before God. Commit your life to Him once more – strengths and weaknesses – good points and bad – asking Him to take what you have and bless it. After all, He created the entire universe from nothing, and He can make something beautiful out of your life.[3]

MAKING FRIENDS

I am also a teenager, and I have a very hard time making friends. Can you help me learn how to influence people and make them like me?

"The best way to *have* a friend is to *be* a good friend to others." That's a very old proverb, but it's still true. Now let me give you a little clue that will help you deal with people of *any* age. Most people experience feelings of inferiority and self-doubt, as I have described. And if you understand and remember that fact, it will help you know the secret of social success. *Never* make fun of others or ridicule them. Let them know that you respect and accept them, and that they are important to you. Make a conscious effort to be sensitive to their feelings and protect their reputations. I think you'll quickly find that many will do the same for you in return.[4]

PHYSICAL CHANGES: WHAT TO EXPECT

I'm twelve years old and my dad tells me my body will soon change a lot. It's already happened to some of the other guys I know. But I don't understand what's about to happen to me or why. Would you sort of fill me in?

I'd be glad to. The growing process is a wonderful and interesting event. It's all controlled by a tiny organ near the center of your brain called the *pituitary gland*. This little organ is only the size of a small bean, yet it's called the master gland because it tells the rest of your glands what to do. It's the "big boss upstairs," and when it screams, your glandular system jumps. Somewhere within your own pituitary gland is a plan for your body. At just the right time, it will send out chemical messengers, called hormones, which will tell the rest of the glands in your body, "Get moving, it's time to grow up." In fact, those hormones will have many implications for your body during the next few years of your life.

I'm glad your dad told you about the changes soon to occur. There are several reasons why you ought to understand this aspect of physical development. First, if you don't know what is about to happen to your body, it can be pretty terrifying when everything goes crazy all at one time. It's not unusual for a teenager to begin worrying about himself. He wonders, "What's going on here? Do I have a disease? Could this be cancer? Is there something wrong with my body? Dare I discuss it with anybody?" These are unnecessary fears that result from ignorance or misinformation about the body. When young people understand the process, they know that these changes represent normal, natural events which they should have been anticipating. So I'm going to tell you exactly what you can expect in the period of early adolescence. There's just no reason for you to be anxious over these rapid physical changes.

The most important change that you will notice is that your body will begin to prepare itself for parenthood. Now I didn't say that you are about to become a parent (that should be years away), but that your body is about to *equip itself* with the ability to produce a child. That's one of the major changes thaat occurs during this period. The correct name for this time of sexual awakening is *puberty.*

During puberty, you will begin to grow very rapidly, faster than ever before in your life. Your muscles will become much more like those of a man, and you'll get much stronger and better coordinated. That's why a junior high boy is usually a much better athlete than a fifth or sixth grader, and why a high school boy is a better athlete than a junior high boy. A dramatic increase occurs in his overall size, strength, and coordination during this period.

Second, your hair will begin to look more like

the hair of a man. You'll notice the beginnings of a beard on your face, and you'll have to start shaving it every now and then. Hair will also grow under your arms for the first time, and also on what is called the pubic region (or what you may have called the private area), around your sex organs. The sex organs themselves will become larger and more like those of an adult male. These are evidences that the little boy is disappearing forever, and in his place will come a man, capable of becoming a father and taking care of his wife and family. This fantastic transformation reminds me in some ways of a caterpillar, which spins a cocoon around itself and then after a while comes out as a totally different creature – a butterfly. Of course the changes in a boy are not that complete, but you will never be the same after undergoing this process of *maturation* (the medical word for growing up).

These rapid changes are probably just around the corner for you. The frightening thing for some kids is that they occur very suddenly, almost overnight. The pituitary gland quickly begins kicking everything into action. It barks its orders right and left, and your entire body seems to race around inside, trying to carry out these commands.

Everything is affected – even your voice will be different. I'm sure you've noticed how much lower your dad's voice is than your own. Have you ever wondered how it got that way? Was it always deep and gruff? Did it always sound like a foghorn? Can you imagine your dad in his crib as a baby saying "Goo, goo" in a deep voice?

Of course not. He wasn't born that way. His voice changed during puberty, and that's what will happen to yours, too. However an adolescent boy's voice is sometimes an embarrassment to him until this deepening process is finished, because it doesn't sound very solid. It squeaks and screeches and wobbles and cracks for a few months. But again, this is nothing to worry about because the voice will soon be deep and steady. A little time is needed to complete this development of the vocal cords.

Another physical problem occurring with both boys and girls during puberty is fatigue, or lack of energy. Your body will be investing so many of its resources into the growing process that it will seem to lack energy for other activities for a period of time. This phase usually doesn't last very long. However, this tired feeling is something you ought to anticipate. In fact, it should influence your behavior in two ways.

First, you must get plenty of sleep and rest during the period of rapid growth.

Second, the foods you eat will also be very important during adolescence. Your body has to have the raw materials with which to construct those new muscle cells and bones and fibers that are in the plans. It will be necessary for you to get a *balanced* diet during this time; it's even more important than when you were six or eight. If you don't eat right during this growth period, you will pay the price with sickness and various physical problems. Your body *must* have the vitamins and minerals and protein necessary to enlarge itself in so many ways.

These are some of the basic changes you can expect within a few years. And when they have occurred, you will be on your way to manhood.[5]

My name is Kim. I am eleven and am a girl. What changes can I expect to take place? I'm especially interested in menstruation and how babies are made.

A girl's body goes through even more complex changes than those of a boy because it has to prepare itself for the very complicated task of motherhood. The way a woman's body functions to produce human life is one of the most beautiful mechanisms in all of God's universe. Let's look at that process for a moment.

All human life begins as one tiny cell, so small that you couldn't see it without a microscope. This first cell of life is called a zygote, which begins to divide and grow inside the mother's uterus.

The uterus is a special place inside the mother's lower abdomen, or what you may have called the stomach. Actually, it's not in the stomach at all, but below it. The uterus is a special little pouch that serves as a perfect environment for a growing and developing embryo. (An *embryo* is the name for a baby in its earliest stages of development.)

All the baby's needs for warmth and oxygen and nourishment are met constantly by the mother's body during the nine months before his birth. Any little slip-up during those very early days (the first three months especially), and the growing child may die. The embryo is extremely delicate, and the mother's body has to be in good physical condition in order to meet the requirements of the growing child.

In order to meet these requirements, a girl's body undergoes many changes during puberty. One of those important developments is called *menstruation,* which I'm glad you asked about. This is a subject that girls will need to understand thoroughly in the days ahead. Most schools provide this information to girls in the fifth or sixth grade, so what I'll tell you now may just be a review of what you have seen and heard elsewhere. However, I feel it is important for boys to understand this process, too, although they are seldom informed properly.

When a woman becomes pregnant—that is, when the one-celled zygote is planted in her uterus after having a sexual relationship with a man—her body begins to protect this embryo and help it grow. It has to have oxygen and food and many chemicals that are necessary for life. The substances are delivered to the uterus automatically, through the mother's blood. But since the uterus has no way of knowing when a new life is going to be planted there, it must get ready to receive an embryo each month, just in case it happens. Therefore, blood accumulates on the walls of the uterus in order to nourish an embryo if the woman becomes pregnant. But if she *doesn't* become pregnant that month, then the uterine blood is not needed. It is released from the walls of the uterus and flows out through the vagina – that special opening through which babies are also born.

Every twenty-eight days (this number varies a bit from person to person), a woman's body will get rid of this unnecessary blood which would have been used to nourish a baby if she had become pregnant. It usually takes about three to five days for the flow to stop, and during this time she wears a kind of pad or a tampon to absorb the blood.

There are some very important attitudes that I want you to understand through this discussion. First, menstruation is not something for girls to dread and fear. Since the subject of blood causes us to shudder, some girls get very tense over this process happening to them. They start worrying about it and dreading its arrival, and some do not want it to happen at all. But actually, menstruation makes possible the most fantastic and exciting event that can ever occur – the creation of a new human being. What a miracle it is for a single cell, the zygote, to quietly split into two, then four, eight, and sixteen cells, and continue to divide until trillions of new cells are formed! A little heart slowly emerges within the cluster of cells, and begins beating to the rhythm of life. Then come fingers and toes and eyes and ears and all the internal organs. A special liquid (called amniotic fluid) surrounds the baby to protect him from any bumps or bruises the mother might receive. And there he stays for nine months, until he is capable of surviving in the world outside. Then at just the right moment the mother's body begins pushing the baby down the birth canal (the vagina) and into the waiting hands of the physician.

The most beautiful aspect of this incredibly complicated system is that it all works *automatically* within a woman's body. It's almost as though the Master Designer, God Himself, were standing nearby, telling her what to do next. In fact, did you know that this is precisely what happens? We are told by King David, writing in the Psalms, that God is present during this creation of a new life. Let's read his description of that event:

> You made all the delicate, inner parts of my body, and knit them together in my mother's womb. Thank you for making me so wonderfully complex! It is amazing to think about. Your workmanship is marvelous—and how well I know it. You were there while I was being formed in utter seclusion! (Psa. 139:13-15, TLB).

Not only did God supervise David's development in his mother's womb (another word for uterus), but He did the same thing for you and me! He has also scheduled each day of our lives and recorded every day in His book. That is the most reassuring thought that I've ever known!

So you see, menstruation is not an awful event for girls to dread. It is a signal that the body is preparing itself to cooperate with God in creating a new life, if that proves to be His will for a particular woman. Menstruation is the body's way of telling a girl that she is growing up – that she is not a child anymore – and that something very exciting is happening inside.

Now, Kim, please don't worry about this aspect of your health. You will not bleed to death, I promise you. Menstruation is as natural as eating or sleeping or any other bodily process. If you feel you are abnormal in some way – if you're worried about some aspect of menstruation – if you think you're different or that maybe something has gone wrong – or if there's some pain associated with your menstruation or you have any question at all, then muster your courage and talk to your mother or your doctor or someone in whom you have confidence. In about 98 cases out of 100, the fears will prove to be unjustified. You will find that you are completely normal, and that the trouble was only in your lack of understanding of the mechanism.

Now, obviously, other things will begin to happen to your body at about the same time as menstruation. You will probably have a growth spurt just prior to your first menstruation. (Incidentally, the average age of first menstruation in American girls is now about twelve-and-a-half years of age, but it can occur as early as nine or ten years or as late as sixteen or seventeen. The age varies widely from girl to girl.)

During this time your body will become more rounded and curvy like your mother's. Your breasts will enlarge, and they may become sore occasionally (boys sometimes experience this soreness, too). This doesn't mean that you have cancer or some other disease, but simply that your breasts are changing, like everything else in your body. Hair will also grow under your arms, on your legs, and in the pubic region, as with boys. These are the most obvious physical changes which take place, and when you see them happening you can kiss childhood good-bye—it's full speed ahead toward adulthood.[6]

I am thirteen-and-a-half and I haven't started to change yet. I'm shorter and not as strong as most of my friends. And they have voices that are lower than mine. It's embarrassing! I don't even have hair down below yet! Is there anything wrong with me?

No. There is nothing wrong with you. You are just progressing on your own timetable. It's just as healthy to grow up later as earlier, and there's no reason to fear that you will never mature. Just hold steady for a year or two, and then the fireworks will all begin to pop for you, just as for everybody else! I can promise you that this is going to happen. If you don't believe me, take a look at all the adults around you. Do you see any of them that look like children? Of course not. *Everyone* grows up sooner or later.

Certainly it's never much fun to be laughed at by your friends, but if you know you'll be different for only a short time, maybe you can stand it. Most important, don't you be guilty of making another person feel bad about himself if you happen to grow before he does![7]

What are wet dreams that I hear other boys talking about?

Many boys have "wet dreams," or what doctors call *nocturnal emissions*. This refers to the fluid which comes out of a boy's penis occasionally at night. The fluid is called semen, and contains millions of cells so tiny that you can't even see them. One of these cells could become a child if it were injected into a female and combined with her egg cell. (That would compose the zygote which we discussed earlier.) This semen sometimes is released during a nighttime dream; then the boy finds the stain on his pajamas the next morning and begins to worry about what is going on. However, this event is perfectly normal. It happens to almost all boys, and is nothing to worry about. A nocturnal emission is just his body's way of getting rid of the extra fluid that has accumulated.[8]

ON SEX AND MARRIAGE

Can I ask you a question about sex? I want to know more about making babies and all that stuff that my older brother talks about.

That's a very important question, and I'm glad you asked it. As your body starts to change, you'll notice that you're beginning to be more interested in people of the opposite sex. Suddenly girls begin to look great to boys, and the boys start appealing to the girls. How do I know this will happen? How can I predict it so accurately? Because sex will soon become an "appetite" within you. If you missed your breakfast this morning, I can predict that you'll be plenty hungry by two o'clock in the afternoon. You body will ask for food. It's made that way. There are chemicals in your body that will make you feel hungry when you haven't eaten.

In the same way, some new chemicals in your body will begin to develop a brand-new appetite when you're between twelve and fifteen years old. This will not be a craving for food, but it will involve the matter called sex, or the male or female aspects of your nature. Every year as you get older, this appetite will become more and more a part of you. You'll want to spend more of your time with someone of the opposite sex. Eventually this desire may lead you to marriage. Marriage is a wonderful union for those who find the right person. However, let me offer a word of caution on that subject.

One of the biggest mistakes you can make with your life is to get married *too soon*. That can be tragic. I want to stress that point in your mind. For two people to get married before they are ready can be a disaster. Unfortunately, this happens all too frequently. I strongly advise you not to get married until you're at least twenty years of age. *Half of all teenage marriages* blow up within five years, causing many tears and problems. I don't want yours to be one of those broken homes.

Now let me describe for you the feeling that sex will bring in the next few years. Boys will become very interested in the bodies of girls – in the way they're built, in their curves and softness, and in their pretty hair and eyes.

Even their feminine feet may have an appeal to boys during this time. If you're a boy, it's very likely that you will think often about these fascinating creatures called girls, whom you used to hate so much! In fact, the sexual appetite is stronger in males between sixteen and eighteen years of age than at any other age in life.

Girls, on the other hand, will not be quite so excited over the shape and the look of a boy's body (although they will find them interesting). They will be more fascinated by the boy himself—the way he talks, the way he walks, the way he thinks. It you're a girl, you will probably get a "crush" on one boy after another. (A crush occurs when you begin to think that one particular person is absolutely fantastic, and you fantasize about the possibility of being married to that person. It is not uncommon to get a crush on a teacher or a pastor or an older man. Usually crushes are constantly changing, lasting only a few weeks or months before another one takes its place.)

Now we need to talk very plainly about the subject of sexual intercourse, which is the name given to the act that takes place when a man and a woman remove all their clothing (usually done before going to bed) and the man's sex organ (his *penis*) becomes very hard and straight. He puts his penis into the vagina of the woman while lying between her legs. They move around, in and out, until they both have a kind of tingly feeling which lasts for a minute or two. It's a very satisfying experience, which husbands and wives do regularly. You probably already know about sexual intercourse as I described it. But did you know that a man and woman do not have intercourse just to have babies? They do it to express love for each other and because they enjoy doing it. In this way they satisfy each other. They may have sexual intercourse two or three times a week, or maybe only once a month; each couple is different. But this is a fun part of marriage, and something that makes a husband and wife very special to each other. This is an act which they save just for each other.

This appetite for sex is something that God created within you. I want to make this point very strongly. Sex is not dirty and it is not evil. Nothing that God ever created could be dirty. The desire for sex was God's idea – not ours. He placed this part of our nature in us; He created those chemicals (hormones) that make the opposite sex appealing to us. He did this so we would want to have a family of our own. Without this desire there would be no marriage and no children and no love between a man and a woman. So sex is not a dirty thing at all; it's a wonderful, beautiful mechanism, no matter what you may have heard about it.

However, I must also tell you that God intends for us to control that desire for sexual intercourse. He has stated repeatedly in the Bible that we are to save our bodies for the person we will eventually marry, and that it is wrong to satisfy our appetite for sex with a boy or girl before we get married. There is just no other way to interpret the biblical message. Some of your friends may tell you differently in the days ahead. You may hear Jack or Susie or Paul or Jane tell about how they explored each other's bodies. They'll tell you how exciting it was and try to get you to do the same.

Let me state it more personally. It is very likely that *you* will have a chance to have sexual intercourse before you reach twenty years of age. Sooner or later that opportunity will come to you. You will be with a person of the opposite sex who will let you know that he or she will permit you to have this experience. You're going to have to decide between now and then what you'll do about that moment when it comes. You probably won't have time to think when it suddenly happens. My strongest advice is for you to decide *right now* to save your body for the one who will eventually be your marriage partner. If you don't control this desire, you will later wish that you had.

God's commandment that we avoid sexual intercourse before marriage was not given in order to keep us from having pleasure. It was not His desire to take the fun out of life. To the contrary, it was actually His *love* that caused Him to forbid premarital intercourse because so many harmful consequences occur when you refuse to obey Him.

You've probably heard about venereal disease, which is caused from having intercourse with someone who has caught it from another carrier. Syphilis, gonorrhea, AIDS, and other diseases are very widespread today. Our country is having an epidemic of these diseases, and they have a damaging effect on the body if they go untreated. But there are other consequences for those who have premarital sex.

They run the risk of bringing an unwanted baby into the world by this act. When that occurs, they face the responsibility of raising a human being – a little life with all its needs for love and discipline and the stability of a home – but they have no way to take care of him or meet his needs. That is tragic.

But just as serious are the changes that take place within a person's *mind* when he has intercourse outside the bonds of marriage. First, and most important, his relationship with God is sacrificed. Premarital sex is a sin, and a person just can't be friends with God if he is going to continue to sin deliberately and willfully. First John 1:6 says, "If we say we are his friends but go on living in spiritual darkness and sin, we are lying" (TLB). It's as simple as that. Furthermore, nothing can be hidden from God, as you know, because He sees everything.

Sin always has a destructive effect on a young person. But I believe the sin of premarital sex is especially damaging to the young person who engages in it. He or she loses the innocence of youth and sometimes becomes hard and cold as a person. It's also likely to affect his or her later marriage because that special experience, which should have been shared with just one person, is not so special anymore. More than one person has had a sample of it.

So you see, there are many obvious reasons why God has told us to control our sexual desires. What I'm saying is that God has commanded us not to have sex before marriage in order to spare us these many other effects of this sin. In fact, the *worst* consequence is one

I have not mentioned, relating to the judgmen of God in the life to come. We are told very clearly in the Bible that our lives will be laid before Him, and He will know every secret. Our eternal destinies actually depend on our faith in God and our obedience to Him.

I hope this has answered your question. There is so much more I could say if time permitted. Why don't you make a list of additional questions to discuss with your father or youth leader at church?[9]

FACING YOUR FEARS

Is there anything else I need to know about growing up that I haven't thought to ask?

Just that many young people worry about their bodies unnecessarily during this time. These kinds of problems plague them:

1. Are all these changes supposed to be happening?
2. Is there something wrong with me?
3. Do I have a disease or an abnormality?
4. Am I going to be different from other people?
5. Does this pain in my breast mean I have cancer? (Remember, I mentioned that the breasts sometimes get sore during adolescence.)
6. Will I be able to have intercourse, or will there be something wrong with me?
7. Will the boys laugh at me? Will the girls reject me? (It's very common for people to feel they're not going to be attractive to the

opposite sex and that nobody will want them because they are not as pretty or handsome as they wish they could be.)

8. Will God punish me for the sexual thoughts that I have? (I told you that you're likely to think about the opposite sex often during these years. When this happens, you may feel guilty for the thoughts that occur.)
9. Wouldn't it be awful if I became a homosexual? (A homosexual is someone who is not attracted to the opposite sex but who is attracted to the *same* sex. It's a boy's interest in boys or a girl's interest in girls. Homosexuality is an abnormal desire that reflects deep problems, but it doesn't happen very often and it's not likely to happen to you.)
10. Could I get pregnant without having sexual relations? (This is another possibility that some young girls fear—that they could find themselves pregnant even if they haven't had sexual relations. I want you to know that this *never* happens; it's an impossibility. Only one time in all of history did this occur, and that's when the Virgin Mary, Jesus' mother, became pregnant even though she had never had sexual intercourse. Jesus was conceived or planted in her uterus by God Himself. That's the only time in the world's history that a human being has ever been born without the father doing his part by providing half of the cell that becomes the zygote.)
11. Do some people fail to mature sexually?

(Any system of the body can malfunction, but this one *rarely* fails.)

12. Will my modesty be sacrificed? (It's common during the early adolescent years for you to become extremely modest about your body. You know it's changing and you don't want anybody to see it. Therefore, you may worry about being in a doctor's office and having to take off your clothes in front of other people.)

Let me say it one more time: these kinds of fears are almost universal during the early years of adolescence. Nearly everyone growing up in our culture worries and frets over the subject of sex. I want to help you avoid those anxieties. Your sexual development is a normal event that is being controlled inside your body. It will work out all right, so you can just relax and let it happen. However, you will have to control your sexual desires in the years ahead, and that will require determination and willpower. But if you can learn to channel your sexual impulses the way God intended, this part of your nature can be one of the most fascinating and wonderful aspects of your life, perhaps contributing to a successful and happy marriage in the years ahead.[10]

NOTES

DD—*Dare to Discipline,* Tyndale House Publishers, Wheaton, IL, 1970, trade paper.

PA—*Preparing for Adolescence,* Vision House Publishers, Santa Ana, CA, 1978.

SWC—*The Strong-Willed Child,* Tyndale House Publishers, Wheaton, IL, 1978.

CHAPTER 1

1. PA 70-71
2. DD 181-182
3. DD 153-154
4. DD 170-171
5. DD 175-176
6. DD 171
7. DD 155-156
8. DD 171-173
9. SWC 208
10. SWC 208-210

CHAPTER 2

1. SWC 190-192
2. PA 21
3. SWC 87-88
4. PA 27-37
5. PA 49-50
6. PA 52-53

CHAPTER 3

1. SWC 193-194
2. SWC 197-202
3. DD 90-91
4. SWC 203-205
5. DD 125
6. SWC 61-62
7. DD 118-121; SWC 222

CHAPTER 4

1. SWC 223
2. DD 181
3. DD 159-160
4. DD 196
5. DD 194-195
6. DD 171
7. DD 181

CHAPTER 5

1. PA 49
2. PA 69-70
3. PA 28-31

4. PA 35-36
5. PA 66-71
6. PA 71-77
7. PA 79
8. PA 87-88
9. PA 79-86
10. PA 88-90

About the Author

JAMES C. DOBSON, Ph.D., is founder and president of Focus on the Family, a nonprofit organization dedicated to the preservation of the home. His syndicated radio program is heard daily on more than 1,300 stations. Active in government activities since 1980, Dr. Dobson recently served on the Attorney General's Commission on Pornography.

For fourteen years Dr. Dobson served as Associate Clinical Professor of Pediatrics at the University of Southern California School of Medicine and simultaneously was on the Attending Staff of Children's Hospital of Los Angeles in the Division of Medical Genetics.

Dr. Dobson has been published extensively, both in professional journals and books. His best-selling books include *Hide or Seek* and *The Strong-Willed Child*. He has also released two popular film series: "Focus on the Family" and "Turn Your Heart Toward Home."

He and his wife, Shirley, are the parents of two children. The Dobsons live in southern California.